Museum

Robert DiNapoli

Littlefox

PRESS

MUSEUM
Robert DiNapoli

Published by Littlefox Press
PO Box 816
Kyneton VIC 3144

for

Caz, Jon, Mim and Bec

Thanks and Acknowledgements

As ever, heartfelt thanks to my closest readers,
Carolyn Masel, Christine Mathieu and Jill Morrow

and to all who have read and responded to various
poems in this book, especially

Chris Bishop, Kate Burridge, Diana Cousens,
Flynn Howard, Valerie Krips, Gershon Maller,
Katie Mirabella, SueRechter and Richard Wrigley

To work with Littlefox Press and its editor, Christine
Mathieu, has been as great a pleasure as it is a privilege.

Special thanks to Jon DiNapoli for his eloquent cover
artwork. More of his art and animation can be found at
https://jondinapoli.life

And, last but not least, a shout-out to all the participants
in our MLS Refectory sessions, ten years old now and
still going strong!

https://robertdinapoli.com
http://themelbourneliteratureseminars.com.au
bob.dinapoli@yahoo.com.au

How Poetry Foots the Earth

Limb and leaf condense from frozen light
  imprinted on the air by graver's block,
  espaliered in space against the night
that coaxes stars' effusions to the dock
  of generation, love's all-quickening play
  that spins the poet's brain like weather-cock,
till it grow great with word and measured say,
  first caught by troubadours who trace its spoor
  through ripples stirred against the body's stay,
then echoed in the songs of stevedores
  upon the wharf as they load freight in holds
  to voyage past all maps' redacted shores

and be exchanged for merchant's fairy-gold,
illusions spun around the heart's true fold.

Contents

Introduction

1. Child of Adam
2. The Luciferian Brink

THE ORPHIC TURN
   i. Orpheus After Hours 4
   ii. Gnostic Escapade 5
   iii. Dimensions 6
   iv. Epiphanies 7
   v. Nothing to Declare 8
   vi. The Cyber Coast 9
   vii. The Great Default 10
   viii. Time Restored 11

12. Transit Concourse
13. Recalled by the Disconsulate of Dis
14. The Bells
15. Broken Morning
16. The Last Act

OUR LADY OF WAYS
   i. The Liminal Detour 17
   ii. Our Lady of Ways 18
   iii. *Lux Mundi* 19

20. Wayward Tendencies
21. Confusion of Tongues

AFTER THE PARADE
   i. Horoscopy 22
   ii. Pageantry 23

24. *La Vita Nuova*
25. Celestial Navigation
26. Procession of Persons
27. *Geworfenheit in Amerika*
28. Update on Adam's Curse

THE CONTRARY CIRCLES OF
         EFFECT AND CAUSE
   i. Boston Blizzard 33
   ii. Penn Station Concourse 34
   iii. Towson Pastoral 35
   iv. The Bashful Errant 36

37. Qlippoth
38. Fade to Black
39. *Sunne gæð to setle*
40. Intimations
41. The Lookout
42. At the Masque
43. The Brink of Day
44. Aeolian Mode
45. The Tower Incarnadine

IN THE SHADOW OF THAT HIDEOUS STRENGT
   i. Speechless 46
   ii. Babel Tor 47

48. Swedish for Common Sense
49. Grand Designs
50. Los's Other Trades
51. The Parting of Orpheus and Eurydice
52. Syncope
53. Bones of the *Nevi'im*
54. Reckonings
55. The Long Ebb
56. The Moveable Feast of the Shekinah
57. Chronometry
58. The Clew
59. Post Mortem
60. Our Lady of the Waste
61. Dishouseled Sacrament
62. Metamorphoses
63. *Psychopompos*
66. Christ in the Etheric
67. Enantiodromia
68. On Lunar Tides
69. Beyond Srange: November 2022
70. Museum
71. The Long Assignment
72. Fantasia: Against Commodity
74. The Magicians of Advent
75. The Little Red Wagon
77. Ventriloquy
78. Deep Dive
79. Moons
80. Archive
81. *Eva Luna*

Introduction

Museums come in many shapes and sizes: museums of art, of science and technology, of natural history, of interior design, of sport, of philately or numismatics, or of whatever else in the universe of things has taken anyone's notice. The most common notion of a museum will conjure scenes of objects on display, of whatever provenance, extricated from their living implication in space and time to sit still for the contemplation of passers-by. The main business of a museum is precisely that contemplation, which gives the bricks-and-mortar structure its name: it is a place for *musing*, for reflection and rumination, a place where we allow the artefacts of time to play upon our consciousness retrospectively.

The poems gathered here, under the title of *Museum*, constitute a comparable display of artefacts. Personal rather than public: moments of time I have known that, for one reason or another, have grown fixed in memory and stubbornly refuse to be forgotten. Their persistence has eventually demanded verbal shape, which I've done my best to provide. Some address specifically personal experience, others record aspects of the worlds through which such experience has moved.

For me, they all embody a strange parallax of past and present, as an older self pauses at a younger self's elbow like Dickens' Ghost of Christmas Yet to Come. Neither self is quite *me* now, as I stand to ponder the resulting display. I have once or twice viewed reconstructions of a living room or a kitchen from the 1950s or 1960s in a museum setting and seen there familiar items of furniture or appliances from my childhood. Such moments involve recognition, of course, but also a vertiginous estrangement from forms that still lie embedded deeply in a consciousness that once moved among them with no inkling of all the ways it would travel from there to here or from then to now. Those swirls of the familiar and the other resemble dream and waking at the same time, wound round each other like twisted vines. That poised twilight forms its own sky, whence the poems in this collection have descended,

As dew in Aprille,
That fallyt on the gras.[1]

---

[1] See 'Moons' (p. 79)

Child of Adam
Dante in Low-Earth Orbit

I was born in free-fall. Liberty
contracted in my power to consume
the weightless, substanceless commodities
that followed like a cloud, a glittering spume,
ejecta of my exit through the gates
that closed on paradise once I'd been flung
to tumble down the slopes of times and fates
and off true being's edge, where I've since hung,
head cauled by this debris, an awkward pall
of orbital particulates that obscure
my view of purgatory's mountain wall,
where I must find some purchase for my cure.
   A common ill: mortality's attaint
   and hollow cheeks – consumption's long complaint.

The Luciferian Brink

Evicted from my home so long ago,
I've struck across these barren lands to find
that everything I thought I'd left behind
remains an indentation in my soul

as if some reader's hand had bookmarked me
to keep their place in this tale's slow unfold,
now paused between closed covers, put on hold,
suspended in mute subjunctivity

till that hand or another once more reach
to plait this story's stranded follicles
and turn the pages of this chronicle,
that light once more unlock the frozen speech

of characters whose condition I've forgot.
My name shows on the passenger manifest,
but I grope for lines that speak my interest,
aware I've touched this coast before, but not

in present costume, temper, cue or pose,
the script untimely changed, my speeches scored
for other parts I'd conned once, long before
the drop-scenes dropped just as the curtain rose.

So am I prince or pauper? Fool or king?
A comic interlude or dying fall?
If the rest be silence, I've smacked into a wall:
the tunnel entrance painted, stars that spring

behind my skull, once bone encounters stone,
the one empyrean I'll ever reach
by this run's close, till other spotlights bleach
another first-night stage in Lucifer's zone

of unreliable celebrity,
the ego scheming past its reasoned means
to market, self-promote, exploit and preen
till it learn another fall's necessity.

THE ORPHIC TURN

i. Orpheus after Hours

Perhaps he came to sing, but all had left.
   With timing like that, he might seem just a clown.
   His belated voice was not of strength bereft,
but the chairs hung off the tables upside-down
   and he couldn't say just why he'd swung the door.
   He looked but did not see her. With his frown,
he might have seemed to us the janitor
   come to prep the venue for the day
   and night to follow, wholly regular.
With quiet, measured pace he made his way
   along the floor, where phantom couples danced
   like revenants returned from past-times' play;
Did he and she move in that crowd entranced?
   He did not wish to see and looked across,
   lest he cast one more time that fatal glance.

Too late his reticence: the lady lost,
'Eurydice' named only time's long cost.

ii. Gnostic Escapade

Flung to earth's cold floor, with neither map
    nor compass-needle slung to show the way,
    cast from unity to plural hap,
consigned to cobble pieces as he may,
    he has no manual or model's guide
    to show him how it's done, his wits at bay
to answer harsh necessity or decide
    which way to tunnel underneath the wall,
    escape bid from the circumstantial slide.
He undertakes the job beneath the pall
    of karma's scowl and fate's sour smile curled,
    that countenances no one's Hades-crawl,

to work their passage up from underworld,
regain the sky beneath the sun's fierce pearl.

iii. Dimensions

He sings through sky too rare to carry voice,
    adrift beyond the many-coloured dome
    whose glass compresses air and channels choice.
On sea-bird wings he dives and skims the foam
    above an ocean bound by glassy night:
    an albatross, blown far off cliff-top home,
re-learns its songs to navigate aright,
    connecting dots of stars in pictured grace
    of constellations webbed in distant light,
whose map above adorns the earth like lace
    mantilla hung on heaven's raven tress,
    in etheric folds that veil her upturned face.

Thus, slung between abysms, he must guess
the drop before his soul's unfounded ness.

iv. Epiphanies

One day they'll maybe know a far *Shabbat,*
  a hallowed interlude of gift and play,
  that circumscribes a precious garden plot,
entr'acte, by uncharted, winding ways
  of never-was, adjoining might-have-been.
  Mere circumstance and fact lack tongues to say
what may or may not fall from heaven's sheen,
  shekinah-glory high on Sinai's peak,
  where law bit stone behind the cloud's dark screen
and Moses, at the last, was bid to seek
  beneath the trailing hem of wonder's core
  for word and vision full enough to speak

the presence he had met once, long before,
in burning limbs of bush on desert floor.

v. Nothing to Declare

He watched the full moon set as morning rose,
   as night retired before the puissant sun
   that binds horizons round the mind and throws
a lid down on the swirl of dreams that run
   at large in sleep, their play all but forgot,
   all memory confiscated at the one
security check – the self that wakes is not
   the self that flew across those etheric fields.
   Frisked and patted down upon the spot,
he'll hand the guards the gems his pockets yield,
   the contraband he stashed in truant play
   thence stowed in treasuries by reason sealed

against the hope of some uncertain day
when dream might temper reason's rude assay.

vi. The Cyber Coast

The threshing mill-wheels of the internet
  turn algorithmic gears that churn the mire
  of still-born will, suspended at its get
by fairy-screens that heave with dancing fire,
  enticing our vexed senses further in,
  down un-world avenues of mock desire
fine-tuned to twang the wires beneath the skin
  that wind our souls around fixed matter's post.
  Now he can scarcely register the spin
that hurls him back and forth upon the coast
  where heaven heaves its waves upon earth's shore,
  amidst whose surge he flits, an errant ghost,

among like wandering spirits, never sure
how far to trust the water's dancing lure.

vii. The Great Default

The riot of reaction on the right
  sounds Hades' klaxon on the warehouse floor,
  'fulfilment-center' irony, the blight
of get and spend promoting ever more
  black fissures in the ground and sky above.
  Numbers troop across bent backs and score
their cold hegemony, a push and shove
  that bores like spirochetes into spent minds,
  belying thought, imagination, love:
as bodies falter, creation's dance unwinds.
  Machine intelligence of bot and drone
  unpicks the woven skein of scenes and signs

first knit upon the nerves that once we owned,
indentured now to clocks and strapped to bones.

viii. Time Restored

All nature longs against that untold time
  when Orpheus and his Eurydice
  from Hades' depths achieve their long, slow climb,
and he at last might turn to her and see
  that no reflexive gaze has cast her back,
  no acid doubt, no dazed uncertainty.
The gates have always stood there down the track,
  awaiting our awakening to all
  they promise from behind our poor minds' stack
of concepts, fabric pre-cut for a pall
  whose shade denies us sight of wider views,
  past mental lumber-stores of trees whose fall
left Eden's slopes deforested, the true
  enticer coiled deep within our heads.
  Our serpent crown put off, new thought pursues
its own curved ramp up from the Stygian dead,
  a freer play of possibility
  than ever was from any scripture read.

Transit Concourse

Small *She* and smaller *He* were never yours
　　to agonise about. That story's done,
　　time called so long ago, behind shut doors –
where you watch your shadows tilt beneath the sun,
　　whose light first bored the eyes within your head.
　　'Had I but' and 'What I've left undone'
cannot unwind those years' entangled thread.
　　Such impotent regret can only send
　　your heart to sound its depths like sinking lead.
The wider scene is where the wounds will mend:
　　abysses plumbed, surveyed and raised to heights
　　where *She* and *He* approach the final bend
and summit of all signs, forget the sleights
　　of hand and heart dished out by trickster time,
　　as waking spirits poised for further flight.

Recalled by the Disconsulate of Dis

Who speaks for souls who stagger down these roads?
  Bent by karma bundles on their backs,
  like kindling faggots, they bear their outsized loads,
assembled without pruning shear or axe,
  all destined for an etheric combust.
  Untidy fasces, consequential acts
whose laden actors suffer spirit's rust,
  now tumbled in sand-barrels for their scour,
  slow flame soon quenched by earth's dead weight and crust,
the leaden trudge up purgatory's tower,
  shedding fascicles of hefty tomes
  transcribed in dim recall of sweet and sour

choked down while threshed in life's entangled grove,
cut free at last to shine in heaven's trove.

The Bells

The bells that sounded all those years ago
   hang still in their high tower, silent brass,
   cobweb-veiled, too old to tell or toll.
And yet, across the waving leagues of grass
   which lap the world between that then and now,
   what strange attunement brings it still to pass
their voices up from time's deep well should play,
   a carillon from under history's rubble,
   that tower thrust below into the clay,
a subterranean earthen mirror-double,
   whose revenant tones still wring my memories
   like starling murmurations over stubble,

in fields laid fallow, the years' unsettled lees
that answer still to heart's unslaked degrees.

Broken Morning

On Uhtan[1]

Night's black had swiped his study window's square
  a smoky mirror, where his double mused,
  as he did, in some Aztec otherwhere,
eyes raised to meet his own, its face perfused
  with outward dark, that caught and held his mind
  corralled behind his eyes in spiral mews.
The gulf without sought his within, declined
  like verbal stems, first-person conjugate:
  the darkness wore his *I*, a mask refined
through long reflection, encounters at the gate
  of *am* and *not*, deep calling unto deep
  across the surging stream of being's spate.

What if, he wondered, *my image there might creep
away and leave my empty chair asleep?*

---

[1]Old English: 'in the dark pre-dawn'

The Last Act

He sings to empty galleries from a stage
   whose lights were quenched before he took his cue,
   his lines conned from script's annotated page.
Since then he struts and frets his hour with due
   attention paid to diction, breath and tone:
   words pitched into the waiting dark, whose flue
conducts them heavenward through chimney-stone.
   The sanctioned channels proffer no reply,
   the rafters ring unseen, through depths unknown
and he can only fill the gods on high
   with imagined auditors, sprung from his mind,
   who crouch like cats behind the shadows' eye.

He feels their presences, before, behind,
his curtain-call to silent fate consigned.

Our Lady of Ways

i. The Liminal Detour

That paradise behind another's eyes
   proves evanescent does not prove it false.
   Desire unfulfilled calls forth our sighs –
we might feel thick, confusing doors and walls,
   but walls and doors alike both separate
   an inside from an out, and what befalls
between the two will, passing through, dilate
   to labyrinthine indirection's weave:
   every threshold will elaborate
a maze of corridors, a twisted sleeve.
   The limen's unforgiving deity
   will have propitiation ere you leave

the hither shore to try the girdling sea
of heaving, untold possibility.

ii. Our Lady of Ways

Haunting, flaunting your capacity
 to tease my stubborn, hide-bound, time-wound thought
 with avatars of your proximity,
my earliest *madonna*, ever sought,
 no sooner found than lost, my stupid hands
 left grappling with the wind, its passage fraught
with earth that sifts through fingers as fine sands.
 What breath draws from the atmosphere my heart
 recirculates along the body's strands.
We stand entwined in love's most inward art,
 precious and invisible. The lead
 I scrape across this paper plays its part

to trace the blossoms bursting in my head
as posy for your breast, which you have bred.

iii. *Lux Mundi*
The Conjuring Coat of Prospero

You are the ether's quiet glory-sheen,
  the blaze that glances off these mounded snows
  whose drifts obscure and drape what lies unseen
between my mind and all it thinks it knows,
  editing my press along this way
  whose course I can't predict, where sudden blows
of fortune's fitful weathers steer the day
  through hint, surmise – dead reckoning's address
  of circumstances you have put in play,
a slow *pavane*, in unfamiliar dress
  you laid across my shoulders eons past,
  occult attire whose sense evades my guess

from underneath its weight until, at last,
your light dissolves such dressing's plaster cast.

Wayward Tendencies

They had changed their throats and had the throats of birds.
W.B. Yeats, 'Cuchulain Comforted'

It's never been about reality
  as commonly conceived: the iteration
  of thing and thing, the measured quantity
of stuff out there, the watchful border station
  where each arrival must provide a name
  that corresponds to passport declaration.
The world, which can't be held to such a frame,
  incarnates in each head as it desires:
  identities unfold and weave like flame
and will not answer, as some clerk requires,
  to quantised spread-sheet double-entry hooks:
  the mind recoils from metred wage-slave hire.

When the bursars rig the game and cook the books,
best join a stroppy troupe of raucous rooks.

Confusion of Tongues

'You wanted hell, you will get hell'.
> Maj.Gen. Ghassan Alian, Coordinator of Government Activities in the
> Territories , 10 October 2023

'My hope and expectation is there will be less intrusive action'.
> President Joe Biden, 14 November 2023

So spoke the free world's leader, with regard
  to hell's most recent Gazan victory-laps,
  as if such platitude could knit the shards
of smashed-up crockery, strewn among the scraps
  of bodies lit by Alfred Nobel's prize,
  conferred with guilt-regret for all the taps
delivered high-explosively by devise
  of policy that topples every wall.
  'Less intrusive action' tries for nice
to glean among the rubble of ruin's pall.
  But Babel wasn't built in just one day,
  and its builders' chatter shattered at the call

of the only grown-up in the room, whose play
was wiser than their plans' and charts' array.

After the Parade

i. Horoscopy

Perhaps we'll fathom what it's all been for
  once we no longer fuss effect and cause –
  those artefacts of time's elusive spoor
that masquerade as dark, unyielding laws,
  fell sergeants, very strict in their arrest,
  who transport all they seize to lonely shores
of island exile, past horizon's crest
  of individual identity,
  entangled in the heavens' cycling, pressed
in diurnal silks of our nativity,
  our planets' weave of inclination's fate.
  We dance on strings we call activity,

our jiggles only screwing down our state
until we yield, swipe clean the dusty slate.

ii. Pageantry

Go still before the mystery and live:
  breathe deeply of the wind that finds you there
  and wait upon its sense and scents that give
high vision of the upland otherwhere,
  beneath the heavens' vaulting, veined by seams
  of gold not struck in miner's headlamp glare
nor ever panned by prospector mid-stream.
  The sun sounds trumpets from the sky's far edge,
  envelops every eye in heaven's gleam,
foretoken, fanfare, high celestial pledge,
  true gold's processional above earth's crest.
  The solar herald speaks from its high ledge,

its rise and faring forth beyond the west
the single pyre of kindled phoenix-nest.

La Vita Nuova

It seems almost a kind of victory,
　　uncelebrated, small, of no great note
　　to all but me: to love disinterestedly,
without display, heart-skip or clutch of throat –
　　such actors' parts rehearsed upon a stage
　　in self-regarding pity's tattered coat:
hormone-, blood- and flesh-enveloped rage,
　　a sort of fever soul must put aside
　　before its wings can lift it from bone's cage
to sing at heaven's gate, on freedom's glide,
　　affinities once borne like heavy chains
　　in crucible's white heat where iron's tried

to gold of transubstantiated pains
that wash the desert floor with cooling rains.

Celestial Navigation

We must look past these limitary forms
  that shaped our first salutes and beckoning,
  the passing strangeness of those psychic storms
each stirred in each beyond small reckoning.
  Can any understand the secret throes
  souls sound in one another's echoing?
The hidden sympathies and tangled woes,
  the certainties of prior affinities,
  now questioned by time's harried to's and fro's
but never lost: the transitivities
  of *verbum caro factum est* revealed
  in heart's own stubborn lodestone tendencies,

whose needle tells, however well concealed,
the pole that holds its sympathies annealed.

Procession of Persons

The soul contracts into a vivid knot:
  spirit presses, wind from otherwhere,
  and stirs thought's waves to white in turbid clots
like foaming rapids, flushed with churning air.
  Thus trammelled waters rise to higher play,
  their energies hurled down the mountain stair
from heights unguessed, against the skies' display
  of tempers, tenors, sensibilities
  that ride our inward channels' disarray.
Before, behind, we track proclivities,
  nubbins of unfathomed will. Unasked,
  they manifest the self's deep mystery,

wayward beast in Hello, Kitty mask
whose schooling constitutes our utmost task.

Geworfenheit in Amerika[1]

Come to upon the fifty-seventh floor,[2]
  heaped round by all its mountains of excess,
  mockeries of heaven's just-slammed door,
to wake like Satan drowned in hell's duress.[3]
    'That must have been some party!' Swimming heads,
  incapable of thought beneath the press
of karmic hangover, psychic spider webs
    that cling the more with every toss and turn.
  Mid-century American retreads
that squeal around the highway's rubber burn.
  Ward Cleaver's pipe and Beaver's paper route,[4]
  crunched in between the ad-breaks' dull sojourn

amid consumer durables, fairy-loot
condemned to wither, fine-grained carbon soot.

---

[1] See also '*Geworfenheit*: The Gnostic Hotel' in *The Gnostic Hotel* (Littlefox Press, 2021).
[2] i.e. 1957, the year of Sputnik, as well as my birth in the second term of the Eisenhower presidency.
[3] Cf. Book I of *Paradise Lost*.
[4] Father and son from the archetypal U.S. sitcom *Leave It to Beaver*.

Update on Adam's Curse
The Navigator's Son

Even as I've grubbed along the earth,
to earn a scanty salary or crust,
a high harmonic, sounded at my birth,
has rung in all my groping through the dust

of circumstance and body's sodden wool:
Look up, it's always bid, and swung my gaze
whence stars rain down their influential pull,
to read, at first, the ticking nights and days

and then the subtler signs my father learned,
to steer a heavy bomber through the air,
whose cargo sought out anything that burned,
ballistic fall of powers from fate's chair,

now massed and mechanised in threshing gears
of Luvah's press[1] – so named by William Blake
in his dispatches from the outmost tiers
of vision's reach – to ice sad ruin's cake.

---

[1] Luvah is Blake's Zoa who presides over both the creative and
destructive aspects of human passion. His 'wine-press' figures
repeatedly in Blake's prophetic poems as an image of apocalyptic
tribulation and violence.

But Sputnik, in the year I hit the ground,
set new-frontier-speak rhetoric all a-whirl
(Cold War death-wish masked in high resound).
The stars my father shot to comb the world

now seemed to call – *Excelsior!* – to heights
that answered young romantic yearning's call,
and never mind the dodgy clockwork sleights
required to loft such throw-weight up the wall

of gravity's well, translated by von Braun
from Peenemünde's *quid* to NORAD's *quo*,
abetted by LeMay's cigar-chomp brawn
that crisped Hiroshima and Tokyo.

But all I saw was sci-fi pageantry:
Forbidden Planet, *Star Trek*'s masque, a globe
of uncanny vistas, future alchemy
past scope of Prospero's book and staff and robe.

My thoughts turned towards the sciences and arts
mathematical, as stairs that wound above
to heights I longed to own, but found my heart
played truant: the differential push and shove

of higher maths from 1696
had dashed my daydreams smack into a wall –
Newton, Bernoulli and Leibniz laid the bricks –

and Zeno's paradox[1] applied the gall,

infinity always somewhere over a fence,
too high, too quick receding out of reach,
that left me feeling aimless, dull and dense.
So I jumped ship and washed up on a beach

whose sands were ghosted by a hidden choir
that sang of far-off reaches to be seen
from bluffs which overlooked horizon's wire
that sliced blue sky from ocean's heaving green.

I turned my eyes towards the massive base
of cliffs that soared above me out of sight,
their flanks hewn by the winds' and waters' race,
their cloud-topped peaks arrayed to left and right

along an endless coast, as if to say
no farther to the sea's scarce-bridled churn.
There, I thought, my questing eye might play
like lighthouse beacon out above the stern

---

[1]Zeno of Elea (495?-430? BCE) proposed that a tortoise, given a head start, could never be overtaken by the fleet-footed Achilles because, by the time he reached the tortoise's starting point, the tortoise would have moved on, however slightly. By the time he reached the tortoise's next position, it would have moved on again, even less, but still a measurable distance, and so on. Its lead would perpetually diminish but could never be reduced to zero. Zeno's reasoning relies on the same parsing of processes into ever more infinitesimal fragments that underlies the conceptual dynamics of the Newtonian/Leibnizian calculus of differential equations, which did my head in as a young physics student.

stochastic thrash of wind and wave below.
I climbed, erratic insect-crawl across
bare stepping stones of ledge and crevice, slow
uncertain navigation of the loss

of bearings I once knew instinctively:
familiar words made strange, strange words made fit
for schemes of meaning unexpectedly
emergent through the mists of being's flit

from covert to apparent verity,
impossible *ex nihilo* reveal
of outward fact or inward certainty
that could belay such climbers' awkward wheel,

slung out above un-meaning's horrid yawn.
Phenomena and *phantasmata* swim
and play together on each other's lawn,
confounding every aspirant in dim

awareness that they must discriminate
the true from false, the better from the worse,
while scenes that pass before them vacillate
in sympathy with Adam's ancient curse.

Thus poetry's defensive rear-guard stand
to lend our harrowed sensitivities
some sense and clarity against the bland
impostures of the dull perversities

that flaunt themselves as know-how, *savoir-faire*,
top-predatory pounce upon the prize
atop the summit of creation's stair,
whence Eve and Adam were tumbled under skies

they had to navigate past death's cold doors,
where only Orpheus could sing his way,
while we negotiate this earth's cold floors,
beneath the press of matter's gravid sway.

The Contrary Circles of Effect and Cause

i. Boston Blizzard
January, 1978

Beneath a sky that brandished bitter snow,
 they'd both returned for Berklee's second term,
 unmoored by disillusion's undertow,
unsure of how that guttered fuse would burn.
 They met, however: conversation's spark
 took fire in head and heart, unfathomed turn,
as either warmed to other in the dark.
 The drifts rose higher, bundled path and street.
 They walked by day, hands clasped and held, the mark
of turnings yet to come, both sour and sweet,
 a revolution neither had foreseen,
 whose course would sling them forward – no retreat –

to other schools and studies in between,
admitting to degrees all unforeseen.

ii. Penn Station Concourse
June, 1978

So like Persephone on her return,
  the rose he held saluted her ascent
  from underneath the Hudson River's bourn.
The crowd rushed by unheeding, whither bent
  no least concern of theirs at this renew –
  fragile, once the destined hours lent
would evanesce like early morning dew –
  but see them now as once they stood embraced,
  one moment out of many washing through
time's weir that speeds and stays. The waters raced
  towards the waiting fall, but left behind
  their spray draped on the air, in rainbow laced

to flutter from the axis of earth's wind,
gonfalon of a heart for life aligned.

iii. Towson Pastoral
May, 1981

One night when grief eviscerated sleep,
   he wandered out and stretched upon the grass
   below his bitter window and the sweep
of summer stars above, whose transits passed
   as he clung to the dirt beneath his spine
   and waited for its press to still his gasps.
He fought the scene whose burst still wrung his mind.
   Too much he'd seen – strange head upon her lap
   where his had lain – atop this very lawn,
whose every blade of dispossession's slap
   made weary mock of heaven's ordered play,
   from which he begged no more than death's swift tap.

Upon his door he'd daubed no lamb's-blood spray,
yet that dark angel spared him as he lay.

iv. The Bashful Errant
December, 2022

At even this ridiculous remove,
   cast forth upon the winds that stir the world,
   what possible conviction could he prove?
What gesture make? What flag could he unfurl
   that might declare his soul's unmoved resolve
   to hold his pointless patch amid the swirl
of hustling mobs and certainty's dissolve,
   declare allegiance to a first-found love
   that swept him up to speed with earth's revolve?
Though long ago the cruder push and shove
   had shouldered them apart and left him stray
   upon some margin, like a guttered glove

let drop by heaven once upon a day,
to lie beneath the stars in night's array.

Qlippoth

In kabbalistic lore, the qlippoth *are vessels shattered by the weight of divine splendour they were placed to contain. Their shards constitute the world of space, time and matter that is the scene of our exile.*

Here, upon this waste of broken jars,
  the *qlippoth* bleed their splendour on the soil,
  shattered vessels, Phaethon's broken cars[1]
that plummeted from higher air's fierce boil.
  Their shards lie darkened in unchanging night,
  dis-hallowed fragments wreathed in shadows' coil.
Burst from within or pitched from lofty height,
  their fall precipitates a true descend
  of sun beneath the earth, forsaken light,
exhausted reservoir whose waters bend
  upon the air more swiftly than rain falls,
  dry beds of mighty rivers' cashed-out wend.

Exposed, stars shine beneath the canyon walls,
glittering stones that strew creation's caul.

---

[1] In the Greek myth, Phaethon comes to grief when he lost control
of his father Apollo's chariot of the sun.

Fade to Black

He cannot see exactly what to do,
  across uncommon times to act his part.
  Too many scripts lie, palimpsests scored through
and over-scrawled by unknown authors' art,
  left strewn across the stage, their sequence tossed
  by heavy feet and undiscerning hearts.
The pageant's yet to pass. Its purpose lost,
  the players march on meanings' broken glints
  that score their eyes with scintillating cost,
the price of long adjournment's guess and hint,
  paths bent upon themselves and rolling back
  to pound the trackless sand to dust and lint,

abandoned portions of the sky's wide track
whose stellar signposts slowly fade to black.

Sunne gæð to setle[1]
The Road of the Dead

We've come this far upon the westward way,
  pursuing rumoured wonders to be found
  beyond what setting sun and stars betray
out past all lights that cross the hither bound.
  Old night has overrun us from behind,
  consumed our shadows leaning on the ground
and trenched the fields with deeper pits that blind
  all eyes that fall into their sullen slots.
  We stumble onward, hoping to unwind
the cerements we trail across these plots,
  our limbs festooned with cobweb-cling arrayed
  against the progress of our fitful trots

toward the bluffs across whose heights day's fade
still plays in hues of opal, pearl and jade.

---

[1] OE: 'the sun goes to its rest'

Intimations

Reality is not a crop or coin
  to be amassed in sacks of memory.
  It's a riddle whose tricky contours all enjoin
that we partake of their topology,
  dare the maze and there begin to learn
  the ins and outs of truth's ontology,
what to dismiss and what we must discern
  amid the shows and throws of matter's haul,
  the shams and glams of self-wrought surface-churn,
that only long experience and fall,
  patiently and watchfully reprised,
  can lead us through, to doors in solid walls

that open on slow-brightening surmise,
first glimmer of an absolute sunrise.

The Lookout

Amidst so many interrupted dreams,
  to live is partial blessing: hope deferred
  but not denied. The gate to Eden gleams
with seraph-fire, by God's own curse unstirred,
  yet through its bars of adamant still glow
  far scenes untainted by the serpent's word,
encountered now in only dream's brief show,
  enough to light imagination's fire
  with driftwood kindled on this strand below,
where we washed up amidst the weed and mire
  of tidal wrack and shipwreck's flotsam-spoor,
  glad enough like sponges to respire,

but minded of our plunge from heights to floor,
from crow's nest whence we'd glimpsed that farthest shore.

At the Masque

Negation comes too easily. We tip –
   with puckered lips, knit brows and narrowed eyes –
   the sour from the sweet at just one sip.
But affirmation's hard: how gauge the rise
   of winds unlooked-for, be they foul or fair,
   while knowing every breath of endless skies
might harbour boon or bane beneath its air?
   How stand prepared to weather all events?
   The welter of the world's not our affair
to govern as we would: to unsure sense
   both bliss and bale might dance behind one mask.
   Our part's to meet fate's eyes along the fence

and empty to the lees its proffered flask,
not fearing whose dark hand had broached the cask.

The Brink of Day

He cannot say death clarifies, for how
   can he perceive what stands beyond that wall,
   which binds the world encircled in its NOW,
unscaled, unpierced by window, door or hall?
   Imagination's dogged forward cast,
   like catapults and hooks, assails the pall
to find there neither purchase, plinth nor mass,
   no crenellations, towers or enfilade,
   ahead no future, behind no echoed past.
And yet the thought of death, in mind's glissade,
   will grapple with the angel whose light hand
   dislocates hip and sings the soul's aubade:

the song of morning mourning, love's remand,
that bids it empty pockets, turn and stand.

Aeolian Mode

By wide canals of Babylon, the willows
  stand along the waters, hung with lyres,
  as ripples pass beneath the clouds' high billows.
Our harps sway side by side from branches higher
  than thought can compass, of living hands bereft,
  strung with cobwebs, ghosts of severed wires.
Absence magnifies silence, weightless heft
  of time that merely gathers like cold moss
  as fingers fold, relinquishing their deft
command of melody to ocean's toss.
  Perhaps the offshore wind that speeds the gulls'
  aeolian song and outstretched wings might cross

these barnacles that cling to upturned hulls
and card the secret strands of memory's wool.

The Tower Incarnadine

Its heights hinge far horizons of the world,
  anchoring both earth's and heaven's spheres,
  terran and celestial chart-scapes, curled
as maps around its spindle, skyline's weirs
  and nested arbiters of near and far,
  blank cartographic windings, polar piers,
auroral wheels turned underneath the car
  that circumnavigates Ezekiel's head.
  Riders swoop round dance of star and star:
carnival ride and centrifuge of the dead
  that throws the clingy clay off swinging feet
  and readies psyches for new morning's tread,

set down, a little dazed, not yet complete,
in the perilous *siege* of incarnation's seat.

In the Shadow of that Hideous Strength

The shadow of that hyddeous strength,
sax myle and more it is of length.[1]
David Lyndsay, 'The Monarche' (1555)

i. Speechless

A silence has descended all around:
  within, without, the numbed exhaust of thought,
  that's stilled the voices both sides of this ground.
Long scrolls of wire seize tangled language, caught
  in no man's land, while strobing searchlight beams
  play back and forth across the garble, fraught
with ghosts of sense that linger near the seams
  where poise and noise lie jumbled on the earth,
  impossible articulacy of dreams
whose dumb-show mimes reality's wide girth
  that no mind compasses by light of day,
  monstrosity and wonder twins whose birth

exceeds the means of lawful speech and play,
drowning grammar in ocean's hectic spray.

---

[1] A reference to the Tower of Babel

46

ii. Babel Tor

How long can meaning's self endure these palls?
  Words murmurate like starlings: billows turn
  the air in smoky twists, no *logos* calls
imperilled light from under chaos' churn.
  Silence or the muttering of mobs
  the only airs unmastered choirs learn.
The shadow of the booming tower robs
  massed voices of coherence: silent night
  impounding every hymn to star that bobs
above all clenched authoritative might
  and beckons souls beyond tall stone and bar,
  past stay of entropy, inertia, blight,

to sing what moves the sun and other stars
across their stately dance on heaven's spars

Swedish for Common Sense

Each night the mind composes self for sleep,
  flat-packed, tucked and folded into dream.
  Each morning it awakens from the deep
with Allen key, screwdriver and a ream
  of step-by-step assembly ordinals
  that puzzles first, a mystifying scheme
of doctrines pictographed by cardinals
  in camera, IKEA-conclave writ
  that bids the abstract two-dimensionals
rise up to find their third in mitred fit
  of flesh and spirit, joined beneath the sun
  like shelves that hold the books whose contents sit

in minds that wake from pagination's run
to shapely thought from ancient seed-beds sprung.

Grand Designs

Have I done well or ill? Who makes *that* call?
  Not me! Though I have been here all the while.
  It's not as if I had much choice of wall
to pound my head with: brick or fieldstone, tile.
  Once heart says GO, all agency gets tossed,
  no time to fuss about your reno's style.
Design? Don't make me laugh! Or count the cost.
  Beatrician Renovations Inc.
  submit no plans and ruthlessly accost
all pre-existing structures in a blink
  of anarchistic 'make it go away' –
  caboodle, whole megillah, kitchen sink –

all slated for the throes of demo day,
when all will be revealed for builders' play.

Los's[1] Other Trades

He stitches poems upon subjunctive skin,
   to tailor metaphysics like a cloak,
   magician's robe, the conjuring spider's spin
of threads that render circumstance bespoke:
   cool metaphors he fixes to those walls
   for gangways, ports and hatches where the stroke
of lightning swings its thunderbolt to fall
   upon the brassy fittings of his ship,
   whose keel he laid down, shaped by adze and awl,
long lives ago, to plough the ocean's lip,
   its furrow sown with song, the muses' play,
   whose white hair under prow and stern will slip

the verses slung and netted in the spray,
in reticule of rhythm's deft *allée*.

---

[1] The archetypal Zoa of Blake's prophetic books, who embodies
the poetic imagination.

The Parting of Orpheus and Eurydice

His heart outraced his head. To still his dread,
  he turned to look. Her face shot forth no beam
of recognition. 'Who are you?' she said.
It's she but not, he thought. Receding dream,
  a weightless vapour falling from the air.
  She backed into the mists, a fading gleam,
already just an ache he'd have to bear,
  whose maenad throes had minced his heavy flesh
  in time's unwind of hope's ascending stair.
Some stories say that, from his sorrow's thresh,
  his spirit, winnowed free of doubts and sighs,
  flew after hers, renewed their dream afresh,

then fathomed in Eurydice's clear eyes
un-filmed and cleansed of Hades' sooty lies.

Syncope

I can no longer even call your name,
   so thickly do the clouds beset the peak
   where last our words resounded on the same
cold winter air, since when we've learned to speak
   like mountain echoes, whispers valley-wide
   following paths unbodied and oblique,
traversing slopes like vapours of the night
   to fall like dew that wreathes the silent nest
   of lowland meadows, pallid ghost of height
suspended unremarked above travellers' rest,
   who never heard our brief, glad syncope,
   interred archivally in time's deep chest,

where larks swoop after may-fly pageantry
beside the tumble of a shoreless sea.

Bones of the *Nevi'im*

Isaiah's thunder rattles down the years,
  in ears gone dead to articulate report
  of all our crime. Our circumstantial leers
grin apishly on unconstrained disports,
  refuse reply to any wiser call
  to pause, refrain, defer to higher courts
than jungle synods summoned by the fall
  of common good and reciprocity,
  left lying on the far side of the wall.
When all must yield to harsh necessity,
  then power and desire contest the field,
  as numbers crunch and thumbs weigh heavily

on scales once hung to arbitrate fair deal,
now stacked against all innocent appeal.

Reckonings

Belshazzar's Feast

Words come and go, dismiss the scheduled call,
  respect no deadline, answer no decree,
   but rather, splayed graffiti-wise on walls,
their cryptic pyroglyphs spell mystery
  to drunken revellers at empire's feast,
  a disembodied hand's calligraphy,
apocalyptic judgement on the beast
  whose pinwheel eyes can grasp no focal point.
  The palace hearth now smashed, its flames released
across the seven hills, time out of joint
  on Nero's misappropriated lyre,
  oblivious to destiny's appoint

of weathered justice, atmospheric fire
that answers *hybris* on a global pyre.

The Long Ebb

For whom these words, which none is like to see
  while master-minded AI mimics speech?
  Who now intends old language joinery
where poets ply their antique craft to reach
  some way of shaping word and thought to last
  the tumult of the waves on time's long strand,
in twilight spread beneath the shadow cast
  by cloud spun cyber-wise to fix the skin
  of unreflective mind, its sails bound fast
against the spirit's breath that heaves within
  but finds no outlet from the skull's dark cave –
  the shaping of the self to world's spin

no longer fairy-dancing on the wave,
but laid beneath cold matter's stony pave.

The Moveable Feast of the *Shekinah*

Both here and not: has this not been the whole
   of my long chase of everything in motion?
   Down to my *lumpen* I, that holds the sole
fast-anchored self to the floor of matter's ocean,
   a wind-sock flying spirit's unseen race,
   whose gusts inflect my every inward notion.
Give and take, a play of pulse, the trace
   of systole, diastole, vein and artery,
   the back and forth, a *pas-de-deux* whose grace
can look behind, beneath fate's ironies.
   What goes away departs and leaves its scent
   in story, scored in heart and memory,

a lingering *trompe l'oeil*, whose desert tent
enshrines authentic glory, heaven-sent.

Chronometry

Strap hours to your wrist and off you go:
   the clock is ticking, measuring your days
   in pulses struck upon the crimson flow
as soul entwines itself along the stays
   of gravity and time to find its spine
   in bodied mass, where thought will bloom and play
on winds that breathe from elsewhere, self-inclined,
   espaliered to trellis, moored to wall,
   at once aware of life's long, slow decline
against the phototropic solar call
   that beats upon the doors of blood and bone
   and bids you rise beneath the heavens' caul.

You check your baggage back into the loam
and wade the sandy stair up from the foam.

The Clew

A sudden joy, as soon as touched, revoked,
  shocked waking, tossed from adolescent dream –
  broad day unpicks imagination's cloak,
and nightmare promenades along the seam.
  Yet do not mourn to see such hopes rebuffed:
  the first approximation of a gleam
that squeaks around the shoulder of the bluff
  and takes for sun what's winnowed through a chink
  that scrapes its blaze, coronal glory snuffed
like stars whose furies swirl down space's sink,
  the quantum drain that lets few photons through.
  We stare with rash temerity and think

our vision, scraped from heaven's floor, is true,
till second looks and thoughts unhitch the clew.

Post Mortem

Once I have sped, how shall I then express
  my changed condition, how find words to tell
  what scenes accommodate my soul's recess?
Old words, congealed of air and blood that wells,
  might simply settle sodden to the floor,
  too weighted still with clay and Adam's fells
to rap a table or stir a creaking door.
  All clocks disarmed, what aspect, mood or tense
  could flick my verbs with morphologic spoor
once I have stowed my metamorphic tents
  and stepped unveiled beneath the heavens' crease,
  as sky breaks blue and morning dews condense,

unheralded in drops on grass and fleece
to lens in small the rising sun's release?

Our Lady of the Waste

What word for you, who've borne so many names?
  Who've shaped this maze we've wandered all these years?
  A labyrinth of winding twists and frames
whose involutions coil our minds' arrears
  and thread us through the weft of matter's coil.
  Mother, *mater*, matter: psychic tiers
enveloping the soul in time's thick soil,
  ouroborean tunnel through the deeps
  where self seeks self, sunk in the ruck and roil
of circumstantial cross-check, thwart and sweep,
  long quest on which our hearts might intimate
  mere faint resolves, between fantastic leaps

from gaunt surmise to orchard-lush estate,
mislaid since we first staggered out the gate.

Dishouseled Sacrament

Modernity has stood awash in blood
   for all of its long run, a juggernaut,
   a mechanised betrayal of the good
it promised fervently on setting out.
   But all the gadgets and gizmology
   have turned in every user's hand to sprout
dire consequence, death's meteorology
   gone rancid under Ford's and Taylor's eye,
   in heaps of Model T and Zyklon B,
assembly-line mass-manufactured cry
   of life caught in the rolling gears and spray
   of bogus shower heads that mock the lie

of progress, clad in carcinomic gray —
efficiency and order's ghastly play.

Metamorphoses

A higher hilarity answers all the woes,
  but who dare name it in the face
  of women's, men's and children's bitter throes,
who stagger down this catastrophic race?
  What hope we muster serves to blunt the sob
  of time on bodies' deeply bedded trace
of neural chorus, neurasthenic throb
  where world abrades the slough of mind's bright skin.
  Thus we take up our roles, accept the job
of tracing back the threads of fate and sin
  for watchers hid above the heavens' steep:
  those authors tweak the very script we spin
for chuckles as they nudge us though the deep,
  where pantomime will graduate from bray
  of Lucius' donkey-shines[1] to Dante's leap,
Divina Commedia dell'Arte spray
  of living forms that dance a Sarabande
  from metamorphic muck to human clay.

---

[1] See *The Golden Ass* of Lucius Apuleius, a third-century comic novel
that conducts a neo-Platonic meditation of the embodied soul's
misadventures through space and time.

Psychopompos[1]

The severing of all bonds will come to pass
when every speaker's conned his Babel-tongue,
and none will fathom why our plans devolve
unseasonably, with insufficient thought
for who will profit, or who will toil in vain,
despair and die amidst another's surfeit.
No certainty except a master mood
of grim futility that sees all paths
form labyrinthine tangles of suppose –
provisional accommodations of fact,
mere crusts of lived experience
strewn point-to-point across the psyche's skin,
that fail to find sure passage in or out:
a nestled grub ensconced in brittle skull.
Self-exiled to the teeming shoots of time,
where event pursues event, a spectacle
that holds our curious noses to the glass,
all unaware the real show unfolds
along the road that snakes behind our backs.
And so we miss our cues, the prompter's box
untenanted as far as we can see,

---

[1] A 'psychopomp' or 'spirit-guide' (a role sometimes played by
Hermes in ancient Greek tradition), who conducts the newly dead to
their abodes in the next world. I composed '*Psychopompos*' as an item
in my as-yet unfinished book-length collection, *The Tenth Host*, whose
lyrics trace a long narrative involving transactions between disparate
levels of psychological/psychic reality and comprise 'these tales' that
'have taken shape as verse' mentioned at the end of this poem.

and all begin declaiming *ex tempore*.
The results, at best, are mixed, and none can grasp
the author's full intent, while some suspect
they play parts scripted by an idiot,
where blood and thunder mask a vacancy
unplumbed and fathomless beneath their feet.
Uncertain whence we came, we cast about
for signs to tell us of our origins.
From creation myths to genealogies
and genome-readings, surer than the cards
dealt by the gypsy-woman's gold-crossed palms,
we poke and peer and fancy we've unrolled
the backward scroll of all our mysteries.
We like to think we read experience
for what we all agree must be the case,
as when we all assume time's forward pace
progresses at a constant hour per hour,
day per month per year, and further fix
its *backward* retrogression at the same
consistent tick of aggregated instants.
What other tally could sound minds accept?
Thus proximate realities, enthroned
as truths by popular assent, take hold
as 'common sense', what 'everybody knows',
strike roots as axioms we all forget
took hold by a consent we never gave.
'The fields we know' enclose a narrow swath –
visible light's small fraction of the whole
electromagnetic spectrum – fencing out
far larger realms whose denizens impend,

above our heads, behind our backs, just past
the reach of eye or ear, but faintly sensed
as shadows in the mind, its changing skies
and weathers, stirred by powers we've no clue
inflect the tenor of the waking thought
we carelessly presume to be our own.
That's why these tales have taken shape as verse:
for only in such slant-wise, sidelong glance
can we catch any glimmers of those states,
in corner-of-the-eye, quick shadow-falls
that flee as soon as glimpsed, yet their propose
now masquerades as so much that we take
as our own clever monkey-shinery.
So follow me to the fenced-off borderline,
and let's see what these verses might suggest . . .

Christ in the Etheric

Some say the he has merely disappeared,
   no longer visible in time and space
   as we traverse their ructions, having cleared
the stile above the aqueducted race
   of waters that propel the wheel of change
   and turn the mill of stars with measured grace.
But across sad Hamlet's bourn his footsteps range,
   whence he surveys the falling mundane night
   (a twilight deepening beneath the strange
amnesiac shade cast by the Watchers' blight),
   the first to shoulder death's appalling lead
   and round that stormy cape with masts upright
and pennants flown above the sullen heads
   beyond which few now ever raise their eyes.
   Not gone, but lapped in cloth of subtle thread,
tendrils of the etheric domain,
   the resurrection garments of the lanced,
   when time shall turn us back against the grain
of Newton's calculus and Descartes' glance
   along the sight-line optics of the globe,
   past existential tyrannies of chance.

Enantiodromia

One great love fulfilled and one forlorn,
  abandoned at the gates of morning, lost
  the hopes that fled like shrieking ghosts, all worn
the heart that owned no means to front the cost,
  indentured for long years to sterile grief
  deep underneath the river's snow-scape tossed,
even as new spring wove flower and leaf
  along its banks and sun beseeched its ice
  to loose its hold and ripple with relief
towards the sea, below the headlands' rise
  whose brow ignites with sunset's crimson blaze,
  its slow decline sustaining deep surmise

that other worlds extend past circling days,
where faltered songs renew abandoned lays.

On Lunar Tides

Truth is bitter – sits on no one's tongue
　　without a frown of alkaloid recoil,
　　a shocking sense that gravity has sprung
its vines of creeping force from virgin soil
　　to tangle every move you make to rise
　　in nets of futile grapple, freighted toil
whose crates depress the deck towards capsize.
　　Invisible assassins crowd the pier
　　and flicker at the edges of your eyes
to send blue blades through heart's and lungs' mêlée
　　that circulates experience's brew
　　of wish and fact in words' and voices' play,

the bodies heaped with chance-wrought *yea* and *nay*
that govern fates and gates beneath moon's sway.

Beyond Strange
November 2022

Uncanny breakings-up of glacial seams,
  within, without – as mind ransacks the world –
  celestial conjunctions, starry beams
enlaced across the sky, new age unfurled,
  emblazoned by strange portents, ancient taint
  enacted once again, cyclonic swirl
as mind falls free of reason's cool restraint.
  Petrograd, March nineteen seventeen,
  America's republic now detained
in holding cell of social-media spleen,
  between, Eurydice no longer there,
  swiped from my back-turned thought as if a screen

of anaesthetic haze had veiled the air
and left me stilled in tidal ebb of care.

Museum

My heart's gone still at last – don't ask me why –
　　its old haunts empty, shut, dilapidate,
　　its scoops no longer headlines on the fly.
Old crises that crossed continents abate
　　to history's hushed corridors below
　　that thread its archives I interrogate,
a janitor who stirs the dusts that blow
　　in after hours, along the floor's slate grey,
　　beneath the massive metatarsal toe
of brontosaur or mastodon that lay
　　in breathless, dark bituminous suspend,
　　all violence withdrawn below the stay

of tarry time-out, under stars' impend,
whose circuits still wheel high around sky's bend.

The Long Assignment

He will not dwell, yet nor can he forget
   how she processed across his field of view.
   Such images embedding past regret
for roads not taken, choices carried through
   that left past blessing stunned by ironies
   whose tang has not quite faded, weary rue
he scarcely feels along his embassy
   on winter's overtures to spring's withdraw,
   diplomatist's semantic nicety
of periphrasis, circumloquacious straw
   that hangs upon the wind of politesse
   to make a dancer's toe from taurine paw

at earth, whose turns will never speed his press
along the path of her long-since recess.

Fantasia: Against Commodity

These words might never make it into books,
  lined up and price-stamped under POETRY,
  nor ever squirm beneath the knowing looks
of scholars, critical constabulary,
  sharp estimates of second-hand appeal
  when bartered in that market's parity.
But maybe some small portion might congeal
  by chance in someone's memory and hold,
  a chrysalid that clings to being's peel,
up to the threshold of the final cold,
  and there fly loose like moths into the pall
  of eschatology beyond the fold
of history's last jest and port of call,
  from whence it's anchors away on bounding surge,
  past chart's and sextant's reach, outside all walls.
Such withheld words might once again emerge
  from decks below, like lanterns hung from spar
  to comfort souls borne swiftly to the verge
of headland promontory, final bar,
  once rounded never after seen again,
  its silhouette soon merged in twilight's far
encroachment on creation's accident –
  the falls of shape and form, all being's crimp
  that seals the pies of self and other sent
from the *Logos* bakery, *fiat* in the slip

of here and there and now and then, accord
of all that stands alone and won't be flipped
upon the marble of exchange, to score
mere abstract profit, worth sold on the bourse
of ends and outcomes beggared by the poor
assent of inert matter to our worse
intentions, narrow gauge of making's worth,
that calculates all blessing to a curse.

The Magicians of Advent

Each Advent sings the morning of a world
   that rises as another's midnight pales.
  Above their endless road, the heavens twirl
around new bearings, quieting the gales
  of jackdaw chatter stirred by mere events
   that captivate the crowds at Christmas sales.
The magian mind has parsed the times' condense
  behind the hum of headline, rumour, play
  of shadows others take for daylight sense,
long enough to trust the broken day –
  when time is full – will flood the world with light.
  Till then the magi plod their winding way

and dream a swaddled infant in the night
whose coming is the reason of all sight.

The Little Red Wagon

hoc est corpus meum

so much depends
upon

a red wheel
barrow
　　　　　 – William Carlos Williams

My soul's own Radio Flyer sags with age,
　chipped and patched, it's carried me along
　from year to year across the bumpy stage
of earth's uncertain highways, distance wrung
　from wheels of no *Merkabah* chariot,
　no desert tabernacle, earthly bung
of heaven's *influenza*, no tidal knot
　of singularity, no laddered rise
　of Jacob's dream, vehicular gavotte,
St Francis' Brother Ass[1] in steel devise.
　Just a means of getting here to there?
　Of negotiating time's and space's lie
that spreads a treacherous floor, so hard to square
　with all that springs from deeply delved desire?
　The steep descent from etheric repair
to realised intention trips the wire

---

[1] St Francis of Assisi referred to his own body as 'Brother Ass', an affectionate acknowledgement of its slow, sturdy and stubborn utility to the spirit's higher agenda.

75

of fortune's booby traps laid cunningly
   beneath the enfilade of stellar fire,
arrayed athwart our paths, necessity
   made visible in zodiac display –
   marquee emblazoned over tangled destinies.
But my red carriage rolls its trundling way
   beneath the glare of that auroral show,
   its flakes of rust conceding time's betray,
the toll imposed on Adam's clay in slow
   extraction of deep veins of anthracite
   laid down when Death was young – his undertow
had barely just begun its work on site,
   to grind the gears and squeal their tuneless whine,
   to draw the shades that linger past this light.
However worse for wear, this wagon's mine.
   So much depends upon our fates conjoined,
   as we rattle down this winding serpentine.

Ventriloquy

There's still so much to learn of wisdom's fetch
   from verse: how rhythm props the spirit's stay
   and rhyme confers its colour, life and stretch
to meanings hid in words' unbreathed clay.
   We shape delusive mud-pies in such speech
   as weights our current air, semantic splay
of thoughts whose origins evade our reach,
   emerging from our heads as if self-wrought.
   But we ventriloquise, along a beach
where ocean's lappings on the sand are fraught
   in tidal ebbs and flows whose gravity
   speaks measures elsewhere fashioned, echoes caught

in mind's unmeasured inward cavities,
the secret hubs of cosmic axle-trees.

Deep Dive

The Reverse Lotus

So turn to peer into the night, look back:
  see all the unread signposts overhead,
  each foundered in earth's shadow like a sack.
Who gamed the drop and shod your feet with lead?
  weighted for disposal down the chute,
  trussed for quick descent and left for dead,
a lumpen parcel, unaddressed and mute,
  unclaimed by all, save clinging gravity.
  And whence this strange umbilicus? Acute
ascender, lanyard, serendipity,
  a breath-sustaining stem whose blossom's brass,
  whose roots are struck above in levity,
where sun strikes earth through atmospheric glass,
  fed down that slender thread, a spider's stair
  spun spiralling between tall blades of grass,
a funnel-image of the sloping lair
  extruded by each aggregate of mass.
  Proceed among the stones and scuttling pairs
of claws that sieve the depths of this estate.
  Turn again: reprise and leave behind
  the chest you plundered, the gold doubloons and plate,
kick free, exhale, observe the bubbles wind
  beneath you as you corkscrew towards the sky,
  then breach and toss the waters from your mind.

Moons

As dew in Aprille,
That fallyt on the gras.[1]

As old moon sinks towards the rising sun,
   bright droplets cluster, clinging to the grass
   in dews condensed from vapours' airy run.
So mind attracts new thought that threads the pass
   from sleep to waking, dream at once forgot,
   that leaves a lingering taste of night's repast,
a ghost hung on the air, whence we cannot
   retrieve more than the barest crumbs, faint specks
   whose dance contracts our brows before the slot
where recollection pushes at her hex.
   The shining threads of memory unspooled,
   she'll find her banished king and seat him next
upon their dais, from whose height they'd ruled,
   in olden days, their kingdoms far and kind.
   Then heaven would again by heart be schooled
and all the ruthless clocks of fate unwind,
   to send the new moon, slender, fair and light,
   afloat above the sunset's fire, refined
like silver all unveiled of smutch and blight,
   the crescent lady of all heart's desire,
   whose full-moon grace pulls diamonds from coal's night.

---

[1]From 'I Sing of a Maiden' (ca. 1400), a Middle English lyric of Marian devotion.

Archive

Here, along these annotated shelves,
  stands all the order I can bring to bear
  upon the helter-skelter past of selves
that came to strut their hour and fret the air
  with laddered cries and squawks of steep dissent,
  pitched at ramparts deaf to their despair,
whose lofty weight upon their heads is bent.
  They bore an agony of prospects thrown
  by scouring winds of contrary ascent,
whose blasts I've taken, measured, logged and sewn
  in folio and quire now stretched and wound
  in leather-bound ottavos, silent zone
of karmic archive, cryptic, slow impound
  of all that coils unheeded in the shade
  of every act, uncalculated ground,
churned under by the swift, resistless blade
  of fortune's plough, whose furrows twist and turn,
  strange tracks of fate's invisible parade.

Eva Luna

for Caz

You sat by me that long night in the house
of intensive care, where my refashioned heart
kept time, inflected by the surgeon's art
that parted ribs, as stealthy as a mouse,
to nibble Adam's folly from my core,
whose drifted residues had dropped their bulk
that might have left me just self-stranded hulk
for gulls' loud feasting on a desolate shore.
And it was you who kissed me back to sleep
when anaesthesia slipped her hold too soon,
returned me underneath the changeful moon,
whose windings, timed by monitors' slow beep,
    knit sutured wounds against approaching day,
    when we'd take up our mats and walk away.